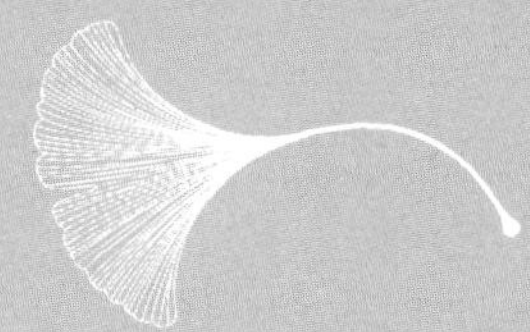

52-WEEK PRAYER PRACTICE FOR WOMEN

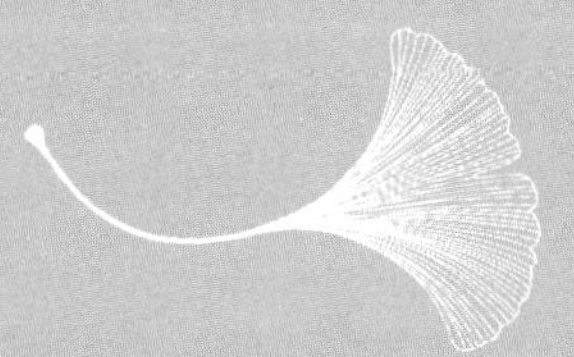

52-WEEK PRAYER PRACTICE *for* WOMEN

Journaling and Devotions to Find Time for Faith

CHELLBEE JOHNSON

Art Directors: Jane Archer & Lisa Schreiber
Art Producers: Megan Baggott & Stacey Stambaugh
Editor: Carolyn Abate & Mo Mozuch
Production Editor: Rachel Taenzler
Production Managers: Lanore Coloprisco & Martin Worthington

Published by Callisto Publishing LLC C/O Sourcebooks LLC
P.O. Box 4410, Naperville, Illinois 60567-4410
(630) 961-3900
callistopublishing.com

Printed and bound in China.
OGP 10 9 8 7 6 5 4 3 2 1

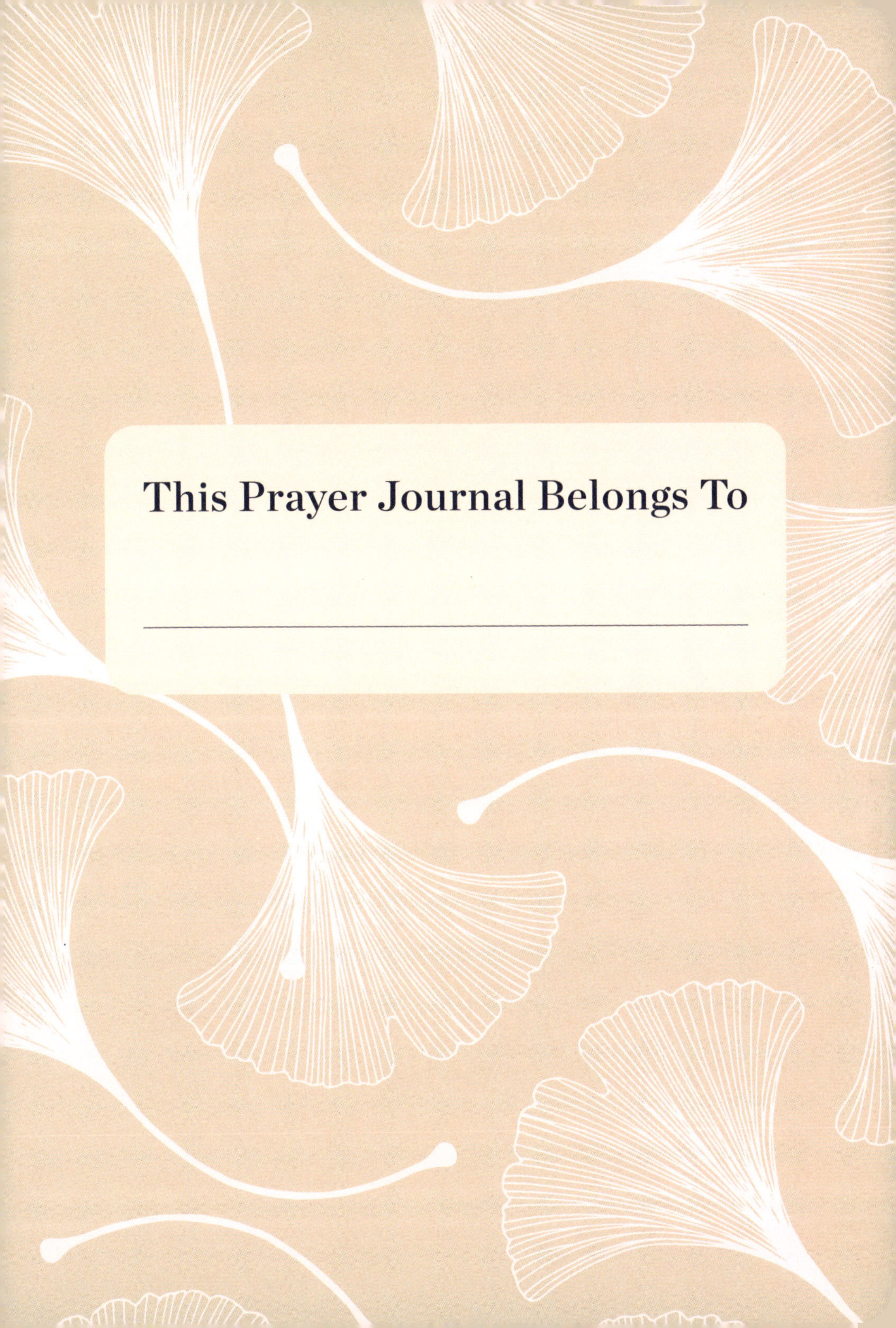

This Prayer Journal Belongs To

____

Contents

Introduction

I am Chellbee Johnson, a daughter of King Jesus, wife, mother, and writer. A few years ago, I shared a prayer I wrote for a friend during a period when she was experiencing anxiety and having thoughts of suicide. I knew the only thing that would get her through this was prayer and scripture. But I didn't want to just pray for her. I also shared with her the prayer and scripture so she could continue to pray over herself. There is power in prayer, and writing your prayer can do so much to help you reflect on all God has done for you.

My goal is for this prayer journal to help you track your prayers, chronicle your testimony, and see your spiritual growth this year. As women, we are often the chief pursuers of Christ in our households, and we face many obstacles. Oftentimes, it can be difficult to continue to have faith and press forward, considering the tribulations, worries, and insecurities we encounter.

That's where this book comes in. I want to help you move forward and stay the course, with your head held high and crown on, because you are everything God says you are.

How to Use This Book

Each week, there will be a theme to contemplate, accompanied by several guided journal prompts and a prayer prompt. Each month, you will find questions for a guided check-in with yourself about your progress.

Tracking your answered prayers will help deepen your relationship with God. I highly suggest you complete the journal from start to finish in order to reflect on each week's and month's themes, answer the tracking questions, and track the prayers that God has answered.

Grab a friend and challenge each other to go through this journal together. I would love to hear about your progress on social media using hashtag #PrayAndPursue

I can't wait to hear about your prayer experience!

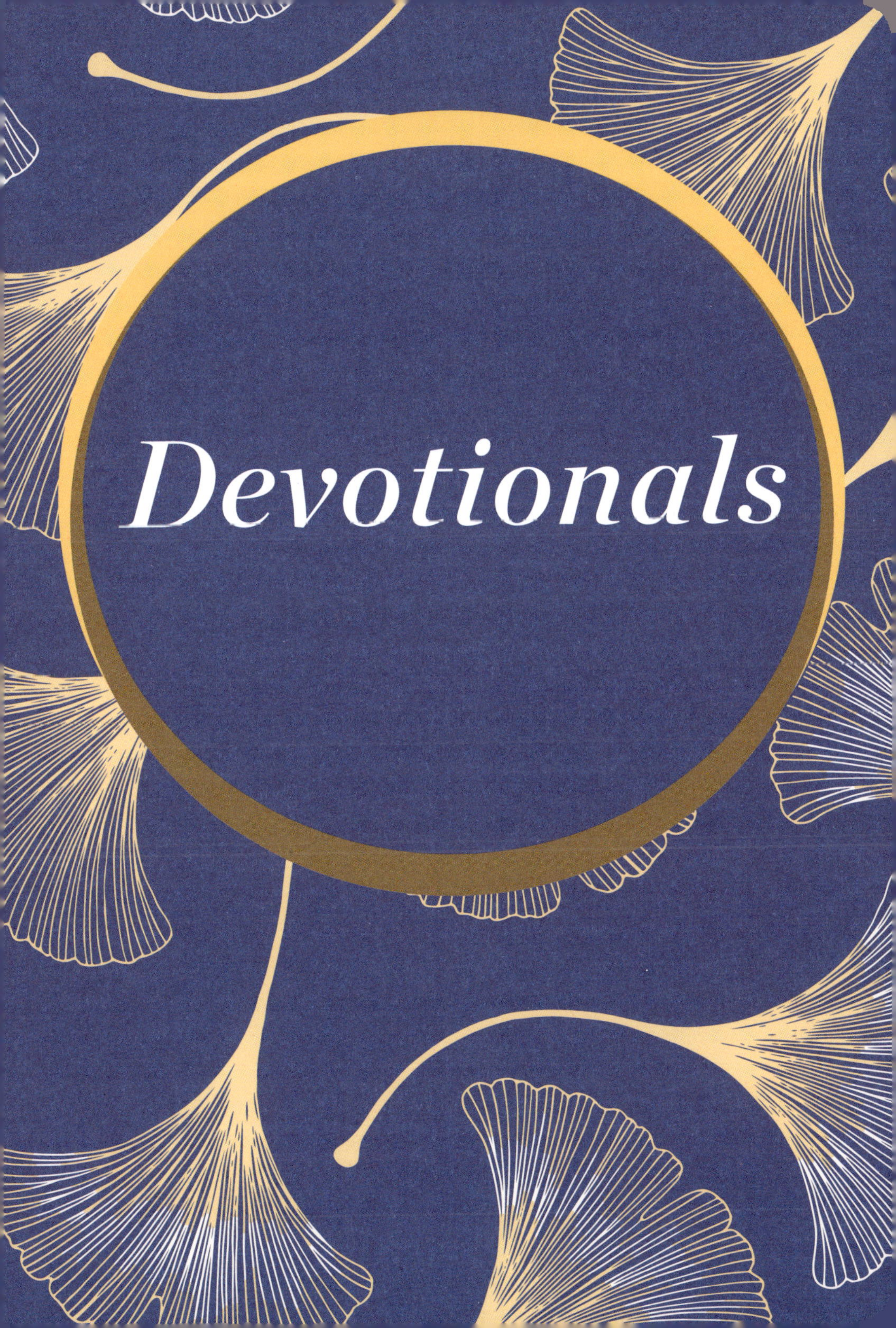
Devotionals

WEEK 1

Faith, Hope, and Patience

Hope helps us continue on in undesirable, challenging, or even tragic circumstances. Take, for example, Africans who were enslaved in the United States. Most of them never saw freedom. None of them lived to see the state of African American life today. But, although they couldn't see what was to come, things did change; hope won out in the end. For a believer, hope is the ability to wait for salvation with joy and confidence. Never stop hoping.

But if we hope for what we do not see, we wait for it with patience. — Romans 8:25 ESV

What are you hoping for right now? What are you asking God for, and how will you maintain that hope in spite of obstacles that may get in your way?

You likely have unanswered prayers that you are waiting on God to fulfill. How will you remain patient and wait on the timing of the Lord?

Write a prayer that helps you stay open to the will of God. Pray that He will ensure the desires of your heart align with His plan for you.

This week, how are you exercising patience?

This week, how has God equipped you to continue pressing forward?

WEEK 2

Pleasing in His Sight

I don't know about you, but I want to be pleasing in His sight. What does that mean, exactly? Imagine this: You begrudgingly empty your overflowing kitchen trash because the last person in your family who put something in the can did not do it. But you still take it out. This to me is a perfect example of being "pleasing in His sight." God knows that you're frustrated about having to perform yet another household chore, but you're doing it anyway. Each day you awake on Earth, God is granting you another opportunity to seek His will. Know that God can see through your actions and into your heart, and use that knowledge to help you make better decisions.

> *Now may the God of peace . . . you with everything good that you may do his will, working in us that which is pleasing in his sight, through Jesus Christ, to whom be glory forever and ever. Amen.* — Hebrews 13:21 ESV

Take a moment to really reflect on yourself, what you do, what you stand for, how you move in this world. Look into yourself, think about the good that is in you, and write about it here.

What steps do you take every day to ensure you are seeking God's will?

Write a prayer thanking God for all the good He has equipped you with. Ask the Lord to deliver you from your shortcomings and give you the discernment to make better choices in the future.

Why is it important to seek God's will?

Think about what steps you can take this week to be even more bold in your faith. Can you be bold in your faith this week?

WEEK 3

Endurance

Going forward each day won't always be easy. Some days may bring considerable pain, tribulation, or isolation. But you must continue forward with faith that God is giving you the endurance and strength to make it through every earthly obstacle. Remember, on the other side of tribulation are blessings, promise, and eternity.

> *For you have need of endurance, so that when you have done the will of God you may receive what is promised.* — Hebrews 10:36 ESV

Why do you think endurance is important as a believer?

Endurance is defined as deliberate purpose and loyalty to your faith, even in trials and suffering. Life is filled with many obstacles, small and large. Write a prayer asking God to give you the endurance to overcome every obstacle in your life and to grant you the wisdom to bring your trials to Him.

This week, what are you doing to learn the promises of God? Write about them here.

What has been your favorite part about this journal so far? What's been the most surprising part of prayer journaling?

WEEK 4

A Child of God

If you have ever watched a toddler, you know they need constant supervision. They don't understand that stoves are hot, that stairs can cause a person to tumble down, or that a street busy with cars is dangerous to cross unless you look both ways. Just like a toddler's caregiver, God is always there to help you in every situation you face. Often, He will provide you with the solution to a problem through His Word or people He has placed in your life. He may provide you with a scripture, show you a lesson, or give encouragement to help you. In whatever way He reaches you, take comfort in knowing He watches over you.

> *See what kind of love the Father has given to us, that we should be called children of God; and so we are. The reason why the world does not know us is that it did not know him.* —1 John 3:1 ESV

How does it make you feel to know God is always right there and ready to help you?

You have been called by His name. What steps are you going to take to be a good example of His name?

Write a prayer asking that God reveal to you scripture that can guide you in every situation, whether it be celebration, victory, heartbreak, or failure.

What did you do this week to ensure and welcome God's divine word and guidance? What are you doing this week to welcome God's correction?

Let's take a minute to do a mental health check-in. How did things go for you this week? How did you feel this week? Were you feeling overwhelmed, stressed, happy, or carefree? Write about your week here.

Equip

What prayers did God answer for you this month?

What have you been praying God would equip you for?

This month, what was the biggest hurdle that God equipped you to overcome?

This month, what are you doing to soak in God's presence?

WEEK 5

God Promised

Let's say you want to become a nurse but have only a high school diploma. Without the time or means to pursue a college education, becoming a nurse may seem unlikely. Scripture tells us Abraham was in a similar situation. God promised Abraham that, at one hundred years old, he would be the father of many nations. Even though it seemed unlikely that he would live long enough to father nations or that his wife, Sarah, would be able to bear a child, Abraham believed because he knew God would fulfill His promise. And He did.

No unbelief made him waver concerning the promise of God, but he grew strong in his faith as he gave glory to God, fully convinced that God was able to do what He had promised. — Romans 4:20–21 ESV

In your life right now, how can you exercise faith like Abraham did?

What steps can you take in your life to grow strong in your faith?

Life is filled with uncertainty. But the Word of God is true. You can trust the promises of God. Write a prayer asking for God's help in strengthening your faith.

How did you exercise faith this week?

This week, evaluate your devotion routine. Do you feel your devotion routine is helping or hindering you from being where you want to be?

WEEK 6

Relinquish It

Relinquishing control to God is necessary for believers. It is one of the hardest things to do—to give up control during difficult times and trust God can handle it. But once you understand that God is in control and has established a plan for you that is better than anything you could imagine, you will relinquish your path for His path.

Jesus looked at them and said, "With man this is impossible, but with God all things are possible." — Matthew 19:26 NIV

In what ways are you seeking God's guidance in your decision-making?

In what area of your life do you feel you need God's help to prepare you for the path ahead?

Write a prayer acknowledging the areas in your life where you need God's help. Ask for God's forgiveness where you have fallen short.

In what ways do you incorporate repentance into your devotion routine?

We've been talking a lot about you seeking forgiveness this week, but did you offer forgiveness to anyone else? Write about it here. How did it feel?

WEEK 7

You Are New

When you give your life to Christ, you are made new. You begin a new life, and the mistakes from your past are forgiven. It is sometimes hard as humans to imagine that God forgives us for our past faults, errors, and sins. But the slate is wiped clean through the redeeming blood of Jesus. Be forever grateful for the perfect love and forgiveness granted through Christ's sacrifice.

> *Therefore, if anyone is in Christ, he is a new creation. The old has passed away; behold, the new has come.* — 2 Corinthians 5:17 ESV

Jesus made you a new creation so that you could return to God. So think for a minute about what the "new you" would like to take full advantage of this week.

The opportunity to start over is no small gift. How does it make you feel to know the sacrifice of Christ has given you the opportunity for a new life?

Jesus paid an expensive price for our salvation. Write a prayer thanking God for the gift of redemption and the new life you have been granted.

Whether you are a new or mature believer, how are you feeling about the new life you have been granted?

Often, we find ourselves shedding certain habits as we deepen our relationship with God. How are you coping with the changes that come with your spiritual growth?

WEEK 8

The Righteousness of God

As believers, we are called to behave righteously. But at the end of the day, believers are human. Let's say, for example, that a company fails to deliver what you've paid for. You might feel the urge to curse out the customer service rep. It's understandable to be extremely frustrated—we've all been there. But even in the face of strong emotions, we are called to follow the path of righteousness and not vent our anger in the heat of the moment.

The anger of man does not produce the righteousness of God. Therefore put away all filthiness and rampant wickedness and receive with meekness the implanted word, which is able to save your souls. — James 1:20–21 ESV

Reflect on a time when you lost your temper and embarrassed yourself. How could you have handled the situation differently?

What do you think "meekness" refers to in this verse?

We all have moments of falling short. But through our prayer and supplication, the Holy Spirit can mature and develop us. Write a prayer for patience, forbearance, and keeping your temper when life does not go as planned.

How can you be mindful during your day to ensure you exercise patience in difficult situations?

How have you felt this week about your growth in your prayer life?

Patience

What prayers did God answer for you this month?

What prayer have you been patiently waiting on God to answer?

Who in your life can use prayer for patience and why?

This month, how will you ensure you continue to pray until something happens?

WEEK 9

Bold Hope

The Lord wants us to know His Word so we can understand the bold hope we have been granted. It's the kind of boldness that allows you to watch the news and see the outcry due to war, famine, and poverty but, because of your faith, still be able to go on.

Since we have such a hope, we are very bold. — 2 Corinthians 3:12 ESV

Reflect on a time you had to overcome a difficult circumstance all by yourself. Now how do you feel knowing you had the mighty Elohim God in your corner?

In this season of your life, how can you be boldly hopeful? Write at least one stretch goal that you want to accomplish in the next year. In bold hope, how will you pursue it?

Know that no tribulations or difficulties we face surprise God. We find rest in the Lord and stay hopeful about our future despite the turmoil we may see. Write a prayer for those living in war zones, the aftermath of a natural disaster, and/or extreme poverty.

How have you felt this week knowing that you and your family are protected because of your faith in Jesus?

What are you doing to create well-rounded devotion time and to find meaningful resources that will help deepen your relationship with the Lord?

WEEK 10

Overcoming

Life is full of tribulations. There will be moments in life of immense pressure and frustration. Your back may be up against a wall, now or in the future, but I encourage you to not cave in to the pressure to cut corners, to pray half-heartedly, to take the easy way out.

I have said these things to you, that in me you may have peace. In the world you will have tribulation. But take heart; I have overcome the world. — John 16:33 ESV

Think about Christ at the end of His earthly life. What does His sacrifice mean to you? How can you honor His decision on a daily basis?

Jesus says that because He overcame the world, so can we, simply because we are believers in Him. Like Christ, how can you find peace and overcome tribulations?

Often, life is a beautiful mess. But somewhere in the midst of the chaos is a glimmer of hope and redemption. Write a prayer asking the Holy Spirit to fill you with the endurance to overcome tribulations.

When you're experiencing a challenging week, what steps do you take to help you reset and find peace? Where or whom do you turn to?

Think about the obstacles you overcame this week. How did it feel knowing you were able to conquer some of them? What about the ones that proved to be too challenging? Write your thoughts here.

WEEK 11

Be Constant in Prayer

Prayer is one of the easiest ways to connect with God. Due to the sacrifice of Christ on the cross, we are able to pray directly to God. Don't let others make you believe prayer needs to be filled with lofty words or can occur only when nothing else is going on. Praying during mealtimes, during the workday, while bathing the kids, or while watching TV is just as important as devotional time. Be grateful for the gift of prayer, and use the power of prayer often.

Rejoice in hope, be patient in tribulation, be constant in prayer. — Romans 12:12 ESV

Reflect on a time when you communed with God. Write about what made you start the conversation. How did He help you commune with Him? How did that experience make you feel?

What was the last prayer God answered for you? Was it for you or someone else? How did it make you feel to know God heard your prayer?

The Bible instructs us not only to pray for ourselves but also to pray for one another. Write a prayer for the first three people who come to your mind.

Being constant in prayer also means praying for others. This week, take a moment to pray for current circumstances in the world.

How can you incorporate regularly praying for others into your devotion routine?

WEEK 12

His Correction Is Equipping You

One of the gifts of the Word is correction. Scripture not only helps us learn who God is but also teaches us what God expects of us so that we can change our behavior and seek His will. No one wants to hear they're doing something wrong. But we're not perfect; we all need correction sometimes. God corrects us so that we can be ready for Him to use us.

All Scripture is God-breathed and is useful for teaching, rebuking, correcting and training in righteousness, so that the servant of God may be thoroughly equipped for every good work. — 2 Timothy 3:16–17 NIV

Reflect on a time when you felt you were being corrected by the Holy Spirit. How did it make you feel?

What do you think you can do differently in your daily routine to apply scripture in your life? Do you think reading scripture daily would help you achieve your goals?

Jesus knew we would experience trials in this life, which is why He left us the Holy Spirit. Write a prayer thanking Jesus for the gift of the Holy Spirit. Ask Him to let you get to know Him through the Word.

How did you feel after prayer this week?

In your alone time with God this week, what has been an ongoing theme, a thought that keeps occurring to you?

Hope

What prayers did God answer this month?

What do you hope to accomplish by completing this journal?

What do you think God wants you to reflect on this month?

What are you praising God for this month?

WEEK 13

Suffering, Then Hope

I often see new believers all too ready to give up their new-found faith and devotion when they're faced with a painful or challenging experience because they expect that once you give your life to Christ, you will be without suffering. The reality is that Christ doesn't offer us a perfect life. But He does offer us hope. In order to discover hope, we must often go through pain and suffering.

> *Not only that, but we rejoice in our sufferings, knowing that suffering produces endurance, and endurance produces character, and character produces hope, and hope does not put us to shame, because God's love has been poured into our hearts through the Holy Spirit who has been given to us.* — Romans 5:3–5 ESV

Why do you think we need to endure suffering to experience hope?

What does *hope* mean to you?

Jesus knew that our lives on Earth would not be without suffering. He doesn't want us to be ashamed; He wants us to learn from our experiences. Write a prayer thanking Jesus for your suffering and the lessons learned through the Holy Spirit.

This week, what situations have developed your character?

This week, what lessons have you learned?

WEEK 14

Dedicate Yourself to the Word

Whom you spend time with is a reflection of your morals and values. The same could be said about what you spend your time doing, reading, and watching. Being mindful of whom you spend your time with and what you spend your time doing are equally important. What you fill your time with will come out in your actions. So be sure to spend time in the Word of Jesus so that you may live it out in your life.

Do not be deceived: "Bad company ruins good morals." —1 Corinthians 15:33 ESV

Think about your day-to-day routine. Whom do you spend time with? What do you spend your time doing?

Who in your life provides comforting and moral company to you?

Don't underestimate the power of influence. The flesh is weak. Write a prayer that you may be filled with the Holy Spirit and have a heart that chases after God.

How are you spending your time this week?

What are you doing this week to incorporate positive influences into your day?

WEEK 15

You Cannot Repay Christ

I'll never forget the images from the movie *The Passion of the Christ*. The graphic detail of the crucifixion of Jesus has always stayed with me. It powerfully depicts events leading up to Jesus's sacrifice: walking past the people while they berated, abused, and humiliated Him, knowing His life would soon end and He would no longer be with His disciples and the people He had dedicated His life to teaching. We can never repay the price He paid on the cross. We may not admit it, but most of us would never even consider giving our lives in such a way, even if it allowed others to be saved.

> *You were bought at a price. Therefore honor God with your bodies.* —1 Corinthians 6:20 NIV

Jesus made the ultimate sacrifice. How are you living a life that honors the price He paid?

___

___

___

What can you do to honor Christ's sacrifice right now?

___

___

___

Write a prayer for the salvation of the loved ones in your life who do not know Christ. Pray that they may be filled with the Holy Spirit and return to their Holy Father, giving themselves back to Christ and honoring the price He paid.

This week, how are you feeling about your spiritual growth?

In what ways are you seeking godly wisdom to handle the obstacles of life this week?

WEEK 16

Be an Internal Beauty

How much time do you spend each day getting dressed, grooming, or pampering yourself? Now think about how much time you spend living in God's Word. If you spend an hour getting ready each morning, then perhaps you can spend just as much time with Jesus. Beauty, looks, and fashion fade, but the Word of God lives forever. It lives in you, the lives you touch, the lives they touch, and so on.

> *Your beauty should not come from outward adornment, such as elaborate hairstyles and the wearing of gold jewelry or fine clothes. Rather, it should be that of your inner self, the unfading beauty of a gentle and quiet spirit, which is of great worth in God's sight.* —1 Peter 3:3–4 NIV

Are you dedicating your time to things that are indicative of the legacy you want to leave?

Be real for a minute. Think about how much time and energy you put into your external beauty and your internal beauty, respectively. Write down your thoughts here.

Write a prayer asking God to show you the natural beauty you have in you. Pray for Him to help you develop your inner beauty so that you may fulfill His purpose for you.

This week, conduct a self-check about where you spent most of your time. Are you happy with the results?

What can you do next week to beautify your internal self? Pray every morning? Write in your journal? List some ideas here.

Fear

What prayers did God answer for you this month?

What is your biggest fear and why?

How are you giving your fears to God?

What was something you did this month that was outside of your comfort zone?

WEEK 17

You Are God's Handiwork

If you're a parent, aunt, cousin, or mentor to young people, you know the feelings you get when you look at the young folks in your life. The admiration and thankfulness you feel for the opportunity to raise them and be a part of their lives is unmatched. That's how God looks at you, with admiration and love. He is grateful that you chose to give your life to Him.

> *For we are God's handiwork, created in Christ Jesus to do good works, which God prepared in advance for us to do.* — Ephesians 2:10 NIV

Reflect on this: God is thankful for you. How does that make you feel?

God regards you as His child, just as He does Christ. Romans 8:17 says you are a co-heir with Christ. What does this mean to you?

Write a prayer acknowledging how grateful you are to be God's handiwork.

This week, during your alone time with God, I want to challenge you to seek to do His good work. What does "doing His good work" mean to you?

This week, take a moment to reflect on what reminded you that you are God's handiwork. Did you have a moment when you just felt like you were His?

WEEK 18

Your Assignments

The grip of anxiety or fear is halting. It can stop you in your tracks and prevent you from taking action. Maybe God is calling you to go to college or start a business, but fear keeps you from applying to school or getting started. We all have an assignment to spread the Good News according to our God-given talents and abilities. Don't let fear keep you from getting started; God has already equipped you with everything you need to do just that.

Casting all your anxieties on him, because he cares for you. —1 Peter 5:7 ESV

What are you worried about right now? How will you give your anxieties to God?

What steps can you take to help you quiet the thoughts of anxiety and fear?

Write a prayer asking God to help you trust the plan He has for you. Pray that He gives you the wisdom to understand what you should be doing to live a life of purpose.

When you think about your purpose, what occurs to you?

This week, what one thing can you commit to doing to spread the Good News? Remember, sometimes ministry begins at home, with our partners and children (or nieces, nephews, or cousins).

WEEK 19

Comparison Is a Trap

Comparison is a trap that we all get ensnared in, even though we know we shouldn't. Social media, with its beautiful depictions of the best parts of people's lives and what they want others to see, has only amplified our fleshly tendency toward comparison. But it doesn't tell the whole story. What no social media post can tell you is what's in the poster's heart and what they're going through. The next time you find yourself comparing your complex life to someone else's social media presence, make a conscious effort to break free of the trap.

Not that we dare to classify or compare ourselves with some of those who are commending themselves. But when they measure themselves by one another and compare themselves with one another, they are without understanding. — 2 Corinthians 10:12 ESV

Make an effort to not let the distraction of comparison trap you. What are you doing to accomplish the assignment God has given you?

Write down ten gifts and talents God has given you.

Rather than comparing yourself to others, spend your time focusing on the race God has set before you. Write a prayer asking God to help you see your worth. There is beauty in the race you were chosen to run.

Before you write down your thoughts about the week, I'd like you to listen to praise music for fifteen minutes. Make a note of how it helped shape your frame of mind.

The only person you are able to truly compete with is yourself. So, with that in mind, what spiritual goals did you lay out for yourself last week, and how well did you fulfill them? What is your spiritual goal this week?

WEEK 20

Understanding the Assignment

There is a peace that comes with understanding who you are in Christ. Spend time in His Word and with Him to help you receive that peace in the most glorious manner. Remember, the world cannot give you the answers. If you spend all your time scrolling social media, watching Netflix, and hanging with friends, then, girl, trust me—you do not understand the assignment.

> *Peace I leave with you; my peace I give to you. Not as the world gives do I give to you. Let not your hearts be troubled, neither let them be afraid.* — John 14:27 ESV

What do you think are the assignments that God has granted you?

How do you go about fulfilling your assignment? How are you seeking God throughout your day?

Write a prayer that you may receive the lesson of Christ Jesus. Not just His lesson but a word just for you to help you through your current season in life.

This week, what can you do differently to keep your spiritual cup full?

How are you seeking the peace of the Lord this week?

Insecurity

What prayers did God answer for you this month?

What has been your biggest insecurity? What about your insecurity has been a blessing?

This month, what are you doing to turn your insecurity into confidence?

What interesting thing has happened to you this month?

WEEK 21

Focus on Right Now

So many people spend so much time living in the past or the future. Often, we can get so worked up worrying about whether something is going to happen, only to have that experience never come. Sometimes we create issues where there are none. But what if you just focused on right now—the tasks and responsibilities of today—and deal with tomorrow when it comes?

> *Therefore do not be anxious about tomorrow, for tomorrow will be anxious for itself. Sufficient for the day is its own trouble.* — Matthew 6:34 ESV

I know your responsibilities are big and your to-do list is never-ending. But what can you do today?

How can you give yourself grace today?

Write a prayer seeking God's grace and help with prioritizing your day. God doesn't want you to be anxious or stressed.

This week, how have you managed your responsibilities to help you have a better day?

This week, what task can you remove from your to-do list in order to spend more time with God?

WEEK 22

What about Your Friends?

Many years ago there was a power song by TLC called "What about Your Friends" about friendship and the importance of having people that you can rely on. Those lyrics still ring so true today. Friendship is about love and acceptance. Real friends are there for you when you're at your best and when you're at your worst. Fear and reproach play no role in lasting friendships.

> *There is no fear in love, but perfect love casts out fear. For fear has to do with punishment, and whoever fears has not been perfected in love.* —1 John 4:18 ESV

Although flesh cannot be held to the standard of Christ, do you think you are the kind of friend you would want in your own life?

How can you create godly friendships that help strengthen your spiritual journey?

Your friendship must be a safe space where you can be yourself freely, without reservations or fear of judgment. Write a prayer for godly, genuine, and mutual friendship.

As important as friendship is, the only thing you can count on in this life is the love of Jesus Christ. How are you affirming Jesus's love for you this week?

What happened between you and your friends this week that reminded you of how much Jesus must love all of you?

WEEK 23

Focus on Him

Don't let the trouble of today cause you to forget the joy and eternal life you have been granted through salvation. Focus your attention on Jesus in times of happiness and in times of trouble, and you will feel the abiding joy that comes from His love.

Fixing our eyes on Jesus, the pioneer and perfecter of faith. For the joy set before him he endured the cross, scorning its shame, and sat down at the right hand of the throne of God. — Hebrews 12:2 NIV

How can you challenge yourself to lean into the love of Christ during trouble? What reminders can you set in place to help you do so?

How can you perfect your faith? What are you doing to elevate and strengthen your faith?

Write a prayer that you can refer to during difficult times, asking the Holy Spirit to help you set your focus on Jesus instead of the trouble of the world. Compared to all He endured so that we may have salvation, we know that our trouble is minor.

This week, focus on joy! What things bring you joy, and how can you do more of them?

How are you feeling this week about the strength of your faith? Do you feel it is growing? Are you still struggling in your faith?

WEEK 24

Your Joy Is in Jesus

Sometimes you might find yourself questioning whether Jesus loves you, wondering if you are favored. I'm here to tell you that you are favored. It might feel silly to say you love someone whom you've never met. But, just as expectant parents love the unborn children they haven't yet met, we love Jesus Christ and He loves us. As you deepen in your love for Christ, you will be filled with so much joy, not based on the world but on gratitude for all the spiritual gifts you have been granted as an heir with Christ.

Though you have not seen him, you love him; and even though you do not see him now, you believe in him and are filled with inexpressible and glorious joy, for you are receiving the end result of your faith, the salvation of your souls. — 1 Peter 1:8–9 NIV

Reflect on a time when your faith was challenged. How did it make you feel? How did you resolve it?

What are you doing to root your joy in Jesus instead of the world?

Christians have been persecuted since the beginning. We are not strangers to having our beliefs challenged, both personally and publicly. Write a prayer that you may have the discernment and strength to overcome Satan's attacks on your spiritual beliefs.

This week, reflect on and write about three spiritual gifts you've received.

This week, find three scriptures on discernment that you can stand on during prayer.

Kindness

How have you focused on kindness during your prayer time?

What prayers about kindness did God answer for your loved ones this month?

This month, how are you ensuring you show kindness to those you encounter?

What makes you feel like you were treated with kindness this month?

WEEK 25

In Everything, Prayer

It's fair to say that for many of us, devotion time is typically the first thing that we place on the back burner when we are busy, stressed, or tired. But I encourage you to not underestimate the power of prayer. Whether it's five minutes or an hour, keep the lines of communication open with God. It's a conversation, after all: talk to Him, listen to Him. Believe me, He will respond.

Do not be anxious about anything, but in everything by prayer and supplication with thanksgiving let your requests be made known to God. — Philippians 4:6 ESV

Reflect on what situation caused you to be anxious this week. How can you transform that anxiety into reconciliation?

Are you grateful for the gift of prayer? How do you express that gratitude to God?

Nothing is too small for God. Write a prayer seeking God's wisdom, teachings, and will in everything that you do.

How are you seeking God in order to keep your anxiety and stress at bay this week?

This week, I want to challenge you to pray three times a day (excluding mealtimes). How did you feel at the end of the week?

WEEK 26

Moving through Fear

Often, we find ourselves afraid or anxious about sharing our God-given gifts. But God has anointed you to use that gift boldly and lovingly to encourage your brothers and sisters in Christ. Even when you feel afraid, you must continue to go forward in faith and boldness. And surrendering your concerns to God can help you.

For God gave us a spirit not of fear but of power and love and self-control. — 2 Timothy 1:7 ESV

Reflect on a time you were fearful about sharing an encouraging word with someone in need. What was the result?

How can you involve God to help you have a spirit of power instead of fear?

We are never truly in control of anything besides our own actions. But fear does not give you permission to opt out of using your God-given talents. Write a prayer to surrender every circumstance to God. I want you to take a picture of it and keep it with you. When you find yourself having a moment of fear, read it.

Think back to the times this week when you felt out of control. In what ways did God help you steer yourself back to some semblance of normalcy?

How is your prayer journaling going? Have you created a routine that allows you to stay consistent?

WEEK 27

Reevaluate Your Way

One of the hardest things to do as a caregiver is to resist the tendency to try to make your child act just as you do. Whether you're a parent, aunt, or teacher, you want the best for those in your care. But the best way isn't always your way. That's not love. Love involves recognizing that those you love have natural gifts, abilities, and attributes that are unique to them.

Love . . . does not insist on its own way; it is not irritable or resentful. — 1 Corinthians 13:4–6 ESV

If you're a parent, how would you describe your parenting style? Are you the kind of parent that you wanted as a kid? Whether you're a parent or not, how can you allow those you love to be themselves with you?

Godly love is nothing like what you learn in the world. It is a welcoming love, patient, kind, and free of judgment. After you read 1 Corinthians 13, how would you define *love* in your own words?

Write a prayer asking God to be the type of parent you desired as a child. Ask God to help you share His perfect love.

What's a memory you have of feeling truly seen and loved for who you are?

Why do you think it is important to not celebrate when others fall short?

WEEK 28

Love Is Patient

This is the kind of love I strive for in my marriage—patient. It's also the type of love I want to share with my children. These aspirations usually leave me riddled with mom and wife guilt. Raising two kids under three years old, working full time, and taking care of a household can be overwhelming. Patience often runs short when you're juggling life.

Love is patient and kind. —1 Corinthians 13:4 ESV

While you strive to love like 1 Corinthians 13:4 says, understand you will fall short at times. How are you giving yourself grace as you strive to love scripturally?

How does your relationship offer you the love described in 1 Corinthians 13:4? What do you think you could do differently to embrace 1 Corinthians 13:4 in your relationship?

Write a prayer asking God to help you in your pursuit to receive and show 1 Corinthians 13:4 love.

This week, what area in your life can you exercise more patience in?

This week, find three scriptures to stand on during prayer about the aforementioned area of your life.

Worth

What prayers did God answer for you this month?

How much do you think you are worth to God?

Who in your life needs God to show them their worth? How can you pray for them this month?

What word of encouragement would you write to your future self?

WEEK 29

Easier Said than Done

We all want to be kind. Most people don't go out of their way to purposely be hateful. When you are forced to deal with someone who is rude or disrespectful, or an adversary, your natural inclination may be to match your enemy's approach. Kindness is easier said than done, as is love. But God is calling you to love everyone, even those who don't have it in their hearts to love you.

But love your enemies, and do good, and lend, expecting nothing in return, and your reward will be great, and you will be sons of the Most High, for he is kind to the ungrateful and the evil. — Luke 6:35 ESV

Why are you choosing to love those who are your enemies?

If the tasks God called us to do were easy, we would not need salvation. How can you love those who challenge, irritate, disrespect, or mistreat you?

Enemies are those who are hateful, opposing, or hostile. The manager who downplays your contributions and that person who vocally disapproves of the choices you make for your family are enemies. Write a prayer that God will give you the strength to love your enemies. Ask God for the discernment to manage these relationships in a godly way.

This week, how are you changing your behavior to ensure you treat everyone with kindness?

This week, how did you feel after encountering an enemy? How did you handle the situation in love?

WEEK 30

Love Freely without Reservations

Love is such a simple concept. But because we're human, it can be one of the most difficult things to do. As you go through life and experience hurt, rejection, and judgment, you begin to fear getting hurt again. But God wants us to love one another freely and without reservation.

We love because he first loved us. —1 John 4:19 ESV

God doesn't expect you to be perfect. He understands you have been hurt. What hurt are you harboring that is making it difficult for you to love others?

Sometimes it is easier to identify how you want to improve when you consider how others may perceive you. No one wants to be considered abrasive. But sometimes life hurts can cause you to act in an abrasive way. How are you treating those you love?

Write a prayer asking God to help you love those close to you, as well as total strangers. Ask that God help you demonstrate Christlike love.

If a stranger were watching you this week interacting with your loved ones, would you be proud of your actions? Do you think your actions reflect the way you want to be loved?

This week, what made you feel loved?

WEEK 31

Let's Start with Love

Have you ever met someone and immediately thought, *They are just not my cup of tea*? Nothing happened, but the two of you seem so different that you don't see how you could ever have anything in common. It is easier to walk away from people than to try to find common ground. As Christians, we all have the same assignment: love. So let's start there when we meet someone who appears to be different from us.

> *For the whole law is fulfilled in one word: "You shall love your neighbor as yourself."* — Galatians 5:14 ESV

Be honest with yourself: How often have you written people off without giving them a chance? What do you think are the implications of being quick to judge others?

How can you love others—friends and strangers—as in Galatians 5:14?

Write a prayer that you may be the type of Christian that you want to meet. Ask God to equip you with a love that bears all things.

This week, how can you be more welcoming to others?

This week, what action can you take that represents Galatians 5:14?

WEEK 32

A Love Bigger than Sin

Even when we are deep in sin, God is trying to get to us. He is trying to show you His love and bring you to His ways. I'm embarrassed to think of God loving me amid my sin—late nights, drinking, and promiscuity. But I know He did. Often I would randomly find myself at church or praying. The Holy Spirit was always right there living in me. He is living in you, too, meeting you where you are.

But God shows his love for us in that while we were still sinners, Christ died for us. — Romans 5:8 ESV

God's love is so perfect and virtuous that it can overpower our fleshly tendency toward sin. Do you remember the moment when you realized God's love for you was real?

Write about a time in your life when you were at your lowest—your "dark hour."

Write a prayer thanking God that His love brought you out of that dark hour. If you are still in your dark hour, pray for the strength to overcome the flesh.

This week, how have you seen God's love for you?

What progress have you made in your spiritual life over the last month?

Love

This month's theme was love. How have you focused on love during your prayer time?

What prayers did God answer for your loved ones this month?

This month, how are you ensuring you show love to those you encounter?

This month, what made you feel loved?

WEEK 33

God Has Gifts Awaiting You

There are so many gifts from God awaiting you. But you have to look for them in the Word and seek them in prayer. Every day.

But the fruit of the Spirit is love, joy, peace, patience, kindness, goodness, faithfulness. — Galatians 5:22 ESV

How can you ensure you seek God's Word to unlock the gifts that await you?

How do you think you can live out the fruit of the Spirit in your life today?

Write a prayer thanking God for the fruit of the Spirit and the opportunity to be more like Jesus.

This week, why do you think being more like Jesus is important?

This week, how has God been faithful to you?

WEEK 34

Keep Your Joy Safe

Do you ever find yourself in a funk, where all you can do is complain? You woke up, you're in good health, you're loved. But for some reason, you can't open your mouth and give God thanks. God knows that if you don't express gratitude regularly, your joy will be stolen.

But thanks be to God! He gives us the victory through our Lord Jesus Christ. —1 Corinthians 15:57 NIV

Romantic movies will have you thinking you should binge-watch sad movies and eat ice cream in a slump. Notice the characters never come out of a self-pity session feeling any better. What do you do when you're feeling down? How does your slump routine help or hinder you?

What can you do differently when you're in a slump to take back your joy and rejoice?

God wants you to give thanks because it will cultivate your faith. After all, you have the gift of eternal life, and isn't that gift enough? Write a prayer that you remain constant in praise, thanks, and prayer.

This week, what area in your life is causing you to gripe and why?

How can you express gratitude despite your circumstances?

WEEK 35

Your Heart Will Rejoice

Sometimes when you really miss someone, the pain can be mingled with positive emotions. Your love for them and the idea of their return fill you with so much joy that you can put aside your current sorrow. This is how we love Jesus.

> *So also you have sorrow now, but I will see you again, and your hearts will rejoice, and no one will take your joy from you.* — John 16:22 ESV

Jesus wants to fill you with a joy that no one can take from you. How does it make you feel to know that Christ wants to fill you with joy?

____

____

____

____

Why do you think finding joy amid tribulations is important?

____

____

____

____

You will forget the pain of this life when you return home to Christ. The gift of eternity outweighs any tribulations you may face on Earth. Write a prayer asking God for the wisdom to rejoice in the gift of eternity.

This week, what did you encounter that caused you sorrow?

This week, what did you encounter that caused you joy?

WEEK 36

Open Up and Praise God

Praising God doesn't have to be complicated. All you have to do to praise God is open your mouth and make a sound. Don't underestimate the power of praising God by making a joyful noise. Whether you're in public or alone, open your mouth in praise through song, prayer, or just a simple "Praise Jesus."

Through him then let us continually offer up a sacrifice of praise to God, that is, the fruit of lips that acknowledge his name. — Hebrews 13:15 ESV

In Black churches, you give God a shout. A shout is a sincere and almost earthshaking praise—you feel it throughout your entire body. When was the last time you lifted your voice in praise?

What does *praise* mean to you? Why do you think praise is important in your devotion time?

Write a prayer that you honor God with your praise. Confess to God anything that you feel is holding you back from praising Him simply for who He is.

This week, how can you incorporate praise into your devotion routine?

This week, what attributes of God did you praise Him for?

Joy

What prayers did God answer for you this month?

What filled your heart with joy this month?

Who in your life is in need of joy? What is your prayer for them?

What area in your life is bringing you joy this month? How can you focus more time on that area?

WEEK 37

Hopelessly Devoted

Sometimes, having multiple big priorities can lead to conflict. For example, have you ever tried to cook dinner and do your job at the same time? Something ends up burned or overcooked every time. After one too many destroyed dinners, I've come to realize it's best to focus on one thing at a time. And so it is with our worship: We should have only one spiritual priority. God wants all your love and praise. He doesn't want to share our worship with another god.

And Jesus answered him, "It is written, 'You shall worship the Lord your God, and him only shall you serve.'" — Luke 4:8 ESV

How can you create a distraction-free devotion time that gives God the praise He deserves?

You cannot love God while worshipping false idols. False idols can be anything or anyone you place before God. Be honest with yourself and evaluate the things you value and prioritize. What things in your life are taking priority over God?

Write a prayer asking that God give you the wisdom to remove anything from your life that inhibits you from serving Him. Ask God to give you a heart that is diligently devoted to Him.

This week, how are you prioritizing God?

This week, what are you doing to devote yourself to being a servant of God?

WEEK 38

Gratitude Breeds Praise

As you grow spiritually, make daily gratitude a part of your routine. You will find it easy to praise God. You will be able to praise God in every circumstance. You will praise God for that pay raise at work or when your children tell you about that poor grade. You will learn to thank God for all things because you trust that God is making everything in your life work together for your good.

Rejoice always, pray without ceasing, give thanks in all circumstances; for this is the will of God in Christ Jesus for you. Do not quench the Spirit. —1 Thessalonians 5:16–19 ESV

Life can be filled with busyness. Take a moment to stop and truly reflect. What are you grateful for? How can you incorporate regular praise into your day?

Think back: When was the last time you rejoiced in the name of the Lord? What does *rejoice* mean to you? Why do you think it is important to pray without ceasing?

Write a prayer asking God that you become fervent in your prayer life. Pray that God gives you the stamina to pray without ceasing.

This week, I want to challenge you to write down one thing each day you are grateful for. How did you feel this week after practicing daily gratitude?

Who in your life are you most grateful for this week? Write a note to the person and explain why you are grateful for them.

WEEK 39

Peace: The Gift That Keeps Giving

The concept of peace can seem elusive if you attempt to define it with a dictionary. Peace in God makes sense only if you believe Jesus died for your sins. You have peace in knowing you have been granted eternal life because you believe in Jesus. You have peace of mind knowing that your home in heaven is awaiting you when your earthly life ends.

> *And the peace of God, which surpasses all understanding, will guard your hearts and your minds in Christ Jesus.* — Philippians 4:7 ESV

Understanding salvation allows you to rest and focus on Christ. Why do you think Christ gave you the gift of peace?

How can you use the gift of peace in your daily life?

Write a prayer that God grant you the peace that surpasses all understanding. Ask for the gift of discernment and wisdom to believe so that you may experience the fullness of Christ Jesus.

This week, how are you seeking peace in your home, marriage, or work life?

What are three activities that help you have a peace-filled day? How can you do these activities regularly?

WEEK 40

Believe in the Unseen

Faith is believing in the unseen. You believe that God created the universe through an utterance. Remember this the next time that you're worried. If you believe that God created the entire universe by uttering a word, then doesn't it seem silly to worry whether it's God's will to provide, protect, and show you your purpose? You *believe*.

> *By faith we understand that the universe was created by the word of God, so that what is seen was not made out of things that are visible.* — Hebrews 11:3 ESV

How does it make you feel to know that God created the universe with an utterance?

Why do you think having faith in the unseen is important as a Christian?

Write a prayer asking God to strengthen your faith. Ask God for the wisdom to understand His power.

This week, reflect on a situation in which you had to have faith in God. What was the result?

Why do you think a life of peace is important as a Christian?

Praise

What prayer did God answer for you this month?

What are you praising God for this month?

How can you magnify God this month and not problems?

How are you celebrating the small wins this month?

WEEK 41

The Battle

Often in television shows, good versus bad is depicted by a little angel versus a devil on the character's shoulder. The battle between flesh and spirit is much like this. However, we have the power through the Holy Spirit to overcome the flesh's tendency toward sin. To harness that power, you need to know the Word of God, pray without ceasing, and be filled by the Holy Spirit.

For to set the mind on the flesh is death, but to set the mind on the Spirit is life and peace. — Romans 8:6 ESV

What do you think "to set the mind on the flesh is death" really means?

Often, we do not live Word-based truth because we don't understand what it means. What does setting your mind on the Spirit look like to you?

Often, you may struggle to overcome the flesh because you don't understand the tools God has provided you with to win the battle. Write a prayer that God equips you to put on the whole armor of God. Stand on Ephesians 6 to write a scripture-based prayer.

This week, how are you harnessing your God-given power to overcome the flesh?

This week, during your prayer time, choose one item to give up, or fast. Consider things you have spent too much time on or indulged in, such as social media or sweets. What are you giving up and why?

WEEK 42

Enlarging Your Faith

In Luke 8:43, there is a woman who had been bleeding for twelve years. She was so desperate for healing that she sought after Jesus, believing that if she simply touched Him, she could be healed. And she was, so much so that Jesus could feel the power that had gone from Him when she was healed. Be desperate for Jesus, and He will enlarge your faith, no matter how small your faith is.

He said to them, "Because of your little faith. For truly, I say to you, if you have faith like a grain of mustard seed, you will say to this mountain, 'Move from here to there,' and it will move, and nothing will be impossible for you." — Matthew 17:20 ESV

Reflect on a time when you were desperate and felt as if you didn't have many options. How did you handle the situation? Do you think it would have been easier to manage if you sought Jesus to enlarge your faith?

Why do you think "faith like a grain of mustard seed" is significant to Matthew 17:20? What does that mean to you?

Matthew says through much fasting and prayer, Jesus will enlarge your faith. Write a prayer asking that God enlarge your faith.

How do you feel after giving up your chosen activity or thing for one week?

This week, how are you exhibiting that nothing is impossible because of your faith?

WEEK 43

Built-In Salvation

Oftentimes, the world teaches that we have to work for everything we want. But as a believer, you know there is no work that grants you salvation. Your salvation is a gift from God simply because you believe in Him and have faith in His Word. There is nothing you have to do or can do that would make you worthy of salvation, because it's already built in.

For by grace you have been saved through faith. And this is not your own doing; it is the gift of God. — Ephesians 2:8 ESV

Why do you think your salvation is not granted based on your work?

Reflect on how it makes you feel to know your salvation is a gift of your faith.

Write a prayer thanking God for the gift of salvation. Express your gratitude that your faith pays the price for salvation.

Understand that grace is a gift from God that is not earned by your work. This week, how are you reframing your perspective on your work?

What steps have you taken this week to strengthen your faith?

WEEK 44

Forgiveness

Accepting responsibility for your misdeeds is never an easy task. Often, we attempt to escape responsibility by pointing our finger at what another person is doing wrong. We have all done it before, right? Your partner, sibling, or co-worker points out an area where you made a mistake, and instead of owning it, you bring up where *they* messed up. And when they fall short, we're all too quick to point it out. What God wants us to do in those moments is not lob accusations but forgive each other.

> *Bearing with one another and, if one has a complaint against another, forgiving each other; as the Lord has forgiven you, so you also must forgive.* — Colossians 3:13 ESV

In Colossians, Paul says we must forgive and put up with one another. How can you implement forgiveness in your life today with the people you interact with regularly?

Why do you think it is important to work together to advance God's Kingdom? What steps are you taking right now to do the work?

None of us are perfect, and in order for the Kingdom of God to advance, we have to work together, forgiving one another our faults. Write a prayer asking God to help you accept others as they are and forgive them for their faults. Ask God that you not magnify others' flaws but magnify the forgiveness we are granted through Christ.

This week, how did forgiveness change you?

What scripture on forgiveness resonates with you? Use it in prayer.

Courage

What prayers did God answer for you this month?

This month, how did you exhibit courage?

What would you say to encourage past you?

Mental health check-in: How are you feeling this month?

WEEK 45

Seek God and Reap the Rewards

You will reap what you sow. If you desire and take action simply for your own gain with no regard to the Holy Spirit and God, you will miss the gift of eternal life. At the core of all, you should seek God and allow the Holy Spirit to lead you. Seeking God is not a chore. You do it because you know that He is worthy and that your life will be better because you serve a mighty God.

> *For the one who sows to his own flesh will from the flesh reap corruption, but the one who sows to the Spirit will from the Spirit reap eternal life.* — Galatians 6:8 ESV

What do you think it means to seek God? What does that look like to you in your everyday life?

How can you sow into the Spirit today?

Often, we think seeking God means we will go without. Matthew 6 says that just as God provides for the birds, He will provide for you. Write a prayer for God to give you the wisdom to seek Him in everything you do.

This week, what seeds did you sow? Be specific.

What can you do differently in your routine to ensure you sow into the Holy Spirit?

WEEK 46

God Washes Us Clean

You're cooking dinner and lose track of time. Next thing you know, you've scorched the pan. It is such a pain to clean burned food off a pan. Often even when you know you've cleaned the pan and removed the burned-on food, it's like you can still see where the food once was. Sin is like scorching the pan. But we are blessed because God washes us clean. Although the flesh is hardwired to sin, God gives us the strength to overcome our flesh through the Holy Spirit.

If we confess our sins, he is faithful and just to forgive us our sins and to cleanse us from all unrighteousness. —1 John 1:9 ESV

Why do you think God's cleansing is important for your salvation? What does it afford you?

Unrighteousness will separate us from God. What does *righteousness* mean to you?

Glory be to God that the residue from sin is removed when God cleanses us. Write a prayer asking God to cleanse you, and express your gratitude for His cleansing you of unrighteousness.

This week, what has been a stumbling block on your path to righteousness?

What steps can you take today to remain cleansed, now and in the future?

WEEK 47

Unforgiveness Hurts Only You

I've seen people hold grudges out of frustration, resentment, and mistrust. But unforgiveness hurts only the person who is holding it. Walking around mad about what someone has done to you doesn't really achieve much. Typically that person has gone on with their life and is not bothered by their actions; meanwhile, carrying that anger is an unnecessary burden for you. The flesh is weak, and people will make mistakes. Forgive them for no other reason than because you need God's forgiveness for *your* shortcomings.

"For if you forgive others their trespasses, your heavenly Father will also forgive you." — Matthew 6:14 ESV

It's simple: You have to forgive if you want God to forgive you. Reflect on a situation in which you have struggled to forgive someone in your life. What about the transgression is giving you pause about forgiving them?

We all make mistakes. Sometimes it is easier to forgive others if you can see the things you have in common. In the prior prompt, you reflected on a situation in which you struggled to offer forgiveness. Have you made similar transgressions? How can you move forward and offer forgiveness freely?

Write a prayer asking for the strength and wisdom to forgive freely and willingly. Ask God for the ability to forgive others in the way that God forgives us.

This week, how are you exhibiting a forgiving heart?

Why do you think forgiveness from God is contingent on you offering forgiveness to others?

WEEK 48

Don't Focus on the Wind

Imagine you're a disciple on a boat in the middle of the water and you see Jesus walking on water. What a sight to see! I often wonder about the courage it took for Peter to step out of the boat and walk to Jesus. Peter had to contend with strong winds as he stepped off the boat. Peter worried about the wind so much that he lost focus on Jesus and almost drowned. Often, we find ourselves in our walk with Jesus focusing on the strong wind instead of Him. But Jesus is still right there to save us from drowning.

But immediately Jesus spoke to them, saying,
"Take heart; it is I. Do not be afraid." — Matthew 14:27 ESV

You don't need to be afraid. Jesus is right there to help you. What are you doing to reach out to Jesus to escape drowning?

How can you gain the courage to walk out of the boat like Peter, to take a leap of faith?

Write a prayer asking for help to focus on Jesus and not on your circumstances. Ask that God grant you the strength to not be afraid.

This week, how did you exhibit courage in the face of strong winds?

What does *courage* mean to you?

Forgiveness

We all make mistakes. What do you need to forgive yourself for this month?

What prayers did God answer for you this month?

What lesson have you learned about forgiveness this month?

What scripture (promise from God) on forgiveness resonates with you that could be used to stand on during prayer?

WEEK 49

The World Goes Silent

Oftentimes, even in a world surrounded by people both in person and online, you can find yourself feeling terribly lonely. For example, let's say you've just received news that you weren't accepted into your dream college. You call up your friends or family to express your sadness and for a word of encouragement, but nobody picks up, leaving you feeling alone with your own thoughts. Well, you'll never get God's voice-mail. He is always there and always available to comfort and listen to you.

So we can confidently say, "The Lord is my helper; I will not fear; what can man do to me?" — Hebrews 13:6 ESV

What can you do differently right now to allow God to be your helper?

Why do you think it's sometimes better to go to God than a friend or family member when you feel sad or frustrated?

You need to understand that God is the best helper. He will never lead you astray, give you bad advice, or tell others your business. Write a prayer asking God for the strength and wisdom to allow Him to be your helper.

Mental health check-in: How did you feel this week? Was this week chaotic, calm, or exciting?

This week, what did you do in moments when you found yourself feeling lonely? How did you overcome those feelings?

WEEK 50

God Is Perfect

God is faithful and forgiving. Even though you are imperfect, God desires a relationship with you. He simply asks that you confess your sins so that you may be cleansed and can therefore be close to him. God is perfect, so He must be separated from sin.

But if we walk in the light, as he is in the light, we have fellowship with one another, and the blood of Jesus his Son cleanses us from all sin. —1 John 1:7 ESV

Why do you think God must be separated from sin?

What obstacle makes it difficult for you to own up to your shortcomings?

It can be scary to fall short. But don't be ashamed to go to God and confess your shortcomings. Write a prayer asking God to help you be bold not only in your prayer life but also in confession. Ask for His help in ensuring that no darkness separates you from Him.

This week, what has God forgiven you for?

How has God been faithful to you?

WEEK 51

Burdens So Heavy

Oftentimes, we are faced with burdens so heavy that we don't know if we are capable of carrying them. And that's why we need to remember that God is here to help us carry whatever we've got. With Him, we can handle it all.

But we are not of those who shrink back and are destroyed, but of those who have faith and preserve their souls. — Hebrews 10:39 ESV

Your knees may be buckling under the weight of your burdens. Remember, God wants to carry your burdens. What burdens do you need to give to God right now?

What are you waiting for God's help with currently?

Life is not easy for anyone. But do not give up your faith. Write a prayer that during every season God will give you the strength to continue forward and have hope.

This week, what are you doing to find the courage to continue forward despite the burdens you face?

Why do you think it is important to cry out to God when you are faced with trials?

WEEK 52

Your God-Given Gifts

One of our obligations as Christians is to leverage our God-given gifts. We have to identify what the Spirit has blessed us with and how we can use it to better the world.

There are different kinds of gifts, but the same Spirit distributes them. There are different kinds of service, but the same Lord. There are different kinds of working, but in all of them and in everyone it is the same God at work. Now to each one the manifestation of the Spirit is given for the common good. — 1 Corinthians 12:4–7 NIV

What gifts has the Holy Spirit given you?

What steps can you take to better leverage your God-given gifts with courage?

Jesus knew we would face ostracism, criticism, and isolation as Christians, which is why He gave us the gift of the Holy Spirit. Write a prayer thanking Jesus for the courage and power that you possess through the Holy Spirit.

What would you like to do differently to improve your alone time with God this week?

What Bible verse are you standing on in prayer this week?

Faith

What prayers did God answer for you this month?

This month, why has maintaining your faith been important?

This month, what are you praising God for?

Who can you pray for in your life who needs help strengthening their faith?

Author Bio

CHELLBEE JOHNSON is an average woman made extraordinary by the loving salvation of Christ Jesus. She is a self-taught Bible student determined to help you chase after the Word of God through prayer and study. She is best known for her Christian lifestyle blog, chellbee.com, where she shares Bible study tips, Bible reading plans, and commentary on how the Bible applies today. She also offers Christian stationery to help busy women like you in their pursuit to stay connected to the Word of God.

NOTES

NOTES

NOTES

NOTES